14.95
11

# SCOTLAND'S LIVING LANDSCAPES

**SCOTTISH NATURAL HERITAGE**

© Scottish Natural Heritage 2003
ISBN 1 85397 349 paperback
A CIP record is held at the British Library
TH3K0403

**Acknowledgements:**

**Author:** John Love (SNH)

**Design and production:** SNH Design and Publications


**Photographs:** Niall Benvie, Laurie Campbell, Sidney Clarke, Adrian Fowles, Lorne Gill/SNH, Digger Jackson, John Love/SNH, Pat and Angus MacDonald/SNH, John Macpherson, Keith Ringland, Margaret Faye Shaw (National Museum of Scotland), Richard Welsby, Ian White/SNH, Steve Whitehorn.


**Illustrations:** Craig Ellery

Scottish Natural Heritage
Design and Publications
Battleby
Redgorton
Perth PH1 3EW
Tel: 01738 444177
Fax: 01738 827411
E-mail: pubs@snh.gov.uk
Web site: http://www.snh.org.uk

Cover photographs (clockwise from top left):
1. Lagandorin, Iona
2. Hougharry, North Uist
3. Oystercatcher
4. Early purple orchid

# MACHAIR

## SCOTLAND'S LIVING LANDSCAPES

by

John Love (Scottish Natural Heritage)

# Contents

Machair flowers, Stilligarry, South Uist

`S i `n tir sgiamhach tir a`mhachair,
Tir nan dithean miogach daithe,
An tir laireach aigeach mhartach,
Tir an aigh gu brath nach gaisear

`Tis a beautiful land, the land of the machair,
the land of the smiling coloured flowers,
the land of mares and stallions and kine,
the land of good fortune which shall never be blighted.

Smeorach Chlann Domhnaill
by John MacCodrum (c1750), North Uist

Red clover

# Introduction

Some 4,500 years ago, a sandstorm overwhelmed a village at the Bay of Skaill in Orkney. People were forced to flee from their houses abandoning most of their possessions. In a hurry to leave through the low door of her home, one woman broke her necklace and left behind on the floor a stream of beads.

In 1850, another storm ripped open the sand dunes to expose some of these houses and later archaeological excavations revealed the best preserved prehistoric village in northern Europe, now known as Skara Brae. But whether the events that led to this ancient settlement being abandoned were quite as catastrophic as the woman's beads imply may be open to question.

Skara Brae is vulnerable to sand blow as it lies on a flat grassy plain just above the beach. This type of landscape is called machair, and is peculiar to northwest Britain. Jarlshof in Shetland, Bosta in Lewis, Northton in Harris, Oronsay off Colonsay, numerous sites recently excavated in South Uist and many other west coast prehistoric settlements are all in similar locations.

Skara Brae, Orkney

1

# What is Machair?

The word 'machair' is Gaelic, meaning an extensive, low-lying fertile plain. Gaelic is not native to Orkney and Shetland but elsewhere 'machair' features in placenames, such as Machrihanish in Kintyre, Machair Bay in Islay, Magheramore and Maghera Strand in Ireland, and in places in the Outer Hebrides. 'Machair' has now become a recognised scientific term for a specific coastal feature, defined by some as a type of dune pasture (often calcareous) that is subject to local cultivation, and has developed in wet and windy conditions. This rather restricts the term to the grassy plain alone. Other authorities prefer to consider the whole system, from the beach to where the sand encroaches on to peat further inland; this is the definition used here.

Machair is one of the rarest habitats in Europe, found only in the north and west of Britain and Ireland. Almost half of the Scottish machair occurs in the Outer Hebrides, with the best and most extensive in the Uists and Barra, and also Tiree. Machair sand has a high shell content, sometimes 80 or 90%. This helps distinguish it from the 'links' of eastern coasts, which are formed from more mineral-based sand.

**Balranald and Hougharry, North Uist**

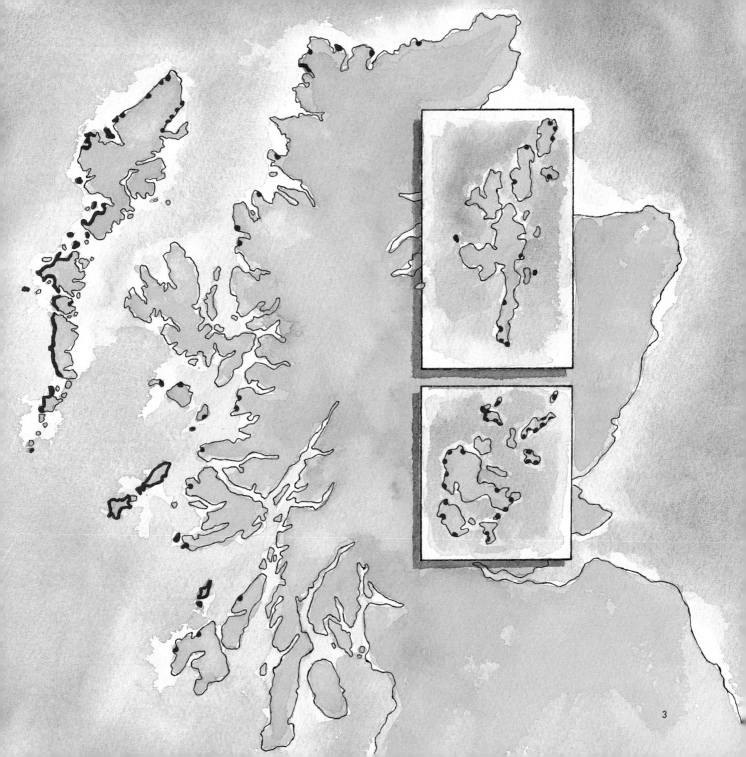

3

# How Machair is formed

The generally received theory of the formation of drift sands and hillocks or downs is this: the fragments of the shells of molluscous animals inhabiting the sea near the coasts, are rolled by the waves toward the shore, where they are further broken and comminuted. . . The wind then blows them beyond water-mark, where, in progress of time, hillocks are formed. These hillocks are occasionally broken up by the winds, and blown inland, covering the fields and pastures. . .

William Macgillivray (1830)

William Macgillivray, who spent much of his youth on the machairs of Northton in Harris, became Professor of Natural History at Aberdeen University. Today scientists might view his remarks as a little simplistic but he is not too far off the mark.

At the end of the last Ice Age, meltwater from the glaciers swept vast amounts of sand and gravel into the sea. The oceans were lower and so the debris was spread over much of what is now the continental shelf. As the sea level rose the glacial sediment - mixed with the crushed shells of masses of molluscs and other marine creatures - were driven ashore by wind and wave action to form characteristic white beaches and coastal sand dunes. The prevailing southwest winds continued to wear away and rebuild the dunes, blowing the light shelly sand over grasslands, marshes and lochs, even reaching the peatland and rocks further inland.

# Cross-section of Machair

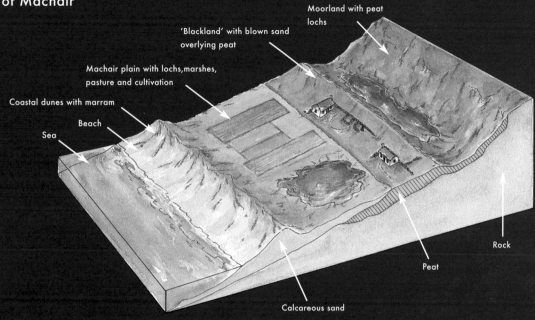

Moorland with peat lochs

'Blackland' with blown sand overlying peat

Machair plain with lochs, marshes, pasture and cultivation

Coastal dunes with marram

Beach

Sea

Rock

Peat

Calcareous sand

Shell sand components, including limpets and sea urchins

Blowing sand, Tràigh Iar, near Hougharry, North Uist

Marram grass, Lingay Strand, Newton, North Uist

Sea-rocket, Tràigh Iar, near Hougharry, North Uist

# Marram

The strandline, highly exposed to wind and wave action, is virtually bare, mobile sand. Only hardy plants like the fleshy-leaved sea rocket and sea sandwort are able to survive. Just above the high-tide mark, where young marram grass begins to take hold, small foredunes begin to develop. With spiky, inwardly-rolled leaves, this grass has a remarkable ability to withstand dry conditions. It thrives upon wind-blown sand and even requires strong winds to break open the seed heads. Its tussocks and deep roots encourage sand to build up and help stabilise the dunes.

Behind such dunes, some up to 10 metres in height, the effects of winds and salt spray are reduced so more plants are able to grow in the bare sand among the marram. Decaying plants hold more moisture and, with less shelly sand being deposited, the soil becomes a little more acid. Marram finally gives way to red fescue and other grasses, mixed in with sand sedge, buttercups, and lady's bedstraw, all of which can still tolerate a thin covering of wind-blown sand in winter.

Sea bindweed

On Ben Eoligarry, Barra, where the sand is blown 100 metres up the rocky slopes inland, there is an unusually abundant covering of primroses.

Sea bindweed has a curious distribution in the Hebrides. It is said to have been introduced by Bonnie Prince Charlie since it grows above the very beach in Eriskay where he stepped ashore in 1745. Somewhat inconveniently, however, it is also recorded from Vatersay, and South Ronaldsay in Orkney; places the Prince never visited!

# Winter

## Natural influences

'In winter, and even until the middle of May, the western division or machair, is almost a desolate waste of sand'

James Macdonald (1811)

Over the last 8,000 years or so, sand blow has been vital in maintaining the machair landscape and many of its characteristic plants. Blowouts and severe erosion can, however, occasionally be catastrophic and Skara Brae vividly demonstrates how dynamic the landscape can be. Even in recent times changes in sea level and climate, or inappropriate land use, can damage the plants that bind the machair, triggering further sand movement.

# Sand and storms

On 19th February 1749, the Reverend John Walker recorded how a hurricane from the northwest, coinciding with high tides, breached an isthmus in Barra, undoubtedly Eoligarry where the airport building now stands. It nearly happened again in 1816.

In 1756 the houses of Baleshare in North Uist were buried in sand up to their roofs. Indeed the name 'Baile sear' means the eastern town, which implies that there would have been a western town 'Baile siar'. The village of Hussaboste is mentioned in a document dated 1389 and was said to have been washed away in the 15th century. It
is remembered locally as an offshore reef just west of Baleshare called Sgeir Husabost, while local tradition maintains how it was once possible to journey across to Heisgeir (the Monach Isles) by horse and cart.

In the winter months large areas of the machair can be flooded, protecting it from wind erosion and also providing good feeding grounds for wildfowl. The machair lochs are rich in nutrients and support an interesting range of water plants (including the rare slender naiad), many invertebrates and large numbers of wintering and breeding waterfowl.

Most machair has formed where it is exposed to the full force of Atlantic storms. Just offshore, dense forests of the seaweed, kelp or *Laminaria* help break up the force of the waves. Every winter huge quantities of battered and broken kelp (often referred to as tangle) are thrown up by the waves and form a natural sea wall along the dune edge. The soft, sandy machair shorelines therefore gain essential protection from this stout leathery seaweed - both living and dead.

Seaweed tangle, Lub Bhan, Benbecula

# Human influences

It must not be imagined that this Hebridean sand is on a barren soil, it being destitute of vegetation only when drifting loose. When in some degree fixed by moisture, or the interspersion of pebbles and shells, it affords excellent crops of barley, when manured with sea-weeds, and its natural pastures are by far the best.
William Macgillivray (1830)

The rich machair grassland behind the dunes appealed to prehistoric settlers. The inhabitants of Skara Brae were Neolithic farmers; sheep and cattle bones have been unearthed from their middens along with the remains of barley. The light sandy soils were easily tilled and ploughmarks have been uncovered in machair, such as near a Neolithic settlement in Westray. These early ploughs would have scratched the surface rather than turn a furrow and it is likely that these early farmers used seaweed as fertiliser.

The machair is still farmed to this day and although agricultural methods have obviously progressed considerably, seaweed is still a vital component. The application of cast tangle before ploughing adds important organic matter to machair soil that not only enriches it but helps to bind it together, hold moisture and resist wind erosion. It is also vital to the long-term stability of the machair pastures. In much the same way, dung from stock, especially cattle, being wintered out on the open machair, helps humus to form.

# The kelp boom

**Mrs Angus Campbell bringing seaweed to spread on the fields - South Uist c1930**

The harvesting and collection of seaweed occurred extensively during the late eighteenth - early nineteenth centuries. The seaweed was burnt to produce a high quality soda ash that could then be used in the manufacture of glass, soap, bleaching agents and gunpowder. During the Napoleonic wars prices peaked at around £25 a ton. Where Clanranald earned only £5,297 per annum in rent from his South Uist tenants, he was making nearly twice that from his kelping enterprise.

Crofters spent more time processing kelp than tending their fields, diverting seaweed from the land to maximise their income. The population of South Uist increased by 200% during the kelp boom, and in Tiree rose from 1509 to 4391!
In 1811 James Macdonald reported how 'the Uists have in many places lost up to one quarter of a mile in breadth by sand drift and sea encroachment'. Exploitation of kelp was exposing the machair to excessive erosion.

# Spring

While May is often the sunniest month in the north and west, it can be dominated by cold easterly winds, so spring comes late to the machair. Dune grassland or links, on the east and south coasts of the mainland, might support hundreds of different plants, yet machair -so much further north - has rather fewer. Nonetheless, a typical patch of machair can look surprisingly rich, with up to 45 species in any metre square.

Once the pasture blooms, it presents an astonishing riot of colour for which the machair is justly famous. It is this beauty that draws many tourists to the Northern and Western Isles each summer and inspired generations of Gaelic bards.

11

Sa mhadainn shamhraidh nuair chinneas seamrag,
`S i geal is dearg air a`mhachair chomhnard.
Is lurach, blathmhor a lusan sgiamhach,
Fo dhriuchd na h-iarmailt `s a`ghrian gan oradh.


On a summer morning when the clover burgeons
Red and white on the level machair,
Lovely the plants with their many blossoms,
Fresh with the dew and shining in the sun.

Oran nam Priosanach
by John Maclean (c1886), Tiree

Irish lady's tresses

Early in the season daisies dust the machair like snow but, in places, they can be a sign of heavy grazing. Other white flowers are eyebrights and wild carrot, with cotton grass in wet areas. In June, yellow is the dominant colour, from buttercups, vetches and bird's foot trefoil. On damper ground, silverweed, yellow rattle, and marsh marigolds thrive. Orkney machair has the rare limestone bedstraw. Red and purple become the main colours later in the summer; red clover and ragged robin, with self heal in damp grassland, while field scabious and autumn gentian are unusually common.

Orchids are particular machair highlights. The rare pyramidal and fragrant orchids both occur in the Outer Hebrides. There is a particular Hebridean type of spotted orchid while a small stretch of North Uist has its own variety of marsh orchid, *Dactylorhiza majalis*

*scotica*, found nowhere else. Irish machair can boast bee orchids, its own variety of marsh orchid and the dense-flowered orchid from the Mediterranean.

There are fewer plants where machair meets moorland, on the so-called 'blackland', and here the croft buildings, enriched pasture and hay meadows are found. On Coll and Barra, however, small patches of damp, peaty pasture or marsh grazed by cattle are home to one of the rarest orchids in Europe; Irish lady's tresses. It is mainly a North American species and how it came to colonise the remote western coasts of Scotland and Ireland is still being debated. One theory is that the tiny seeds were transported on the muddy feet of migrant wildfowl such as white-fronted geese.

Wildflowers, Links of
Sumburgh, Shetland

Yellow rattle

Self heal

Machair, Stilligarry,
South Uist

# Cultivation

. . . these sands produce crops of barley, oats, rye and potatoes, or of natural grass and wild clover, far beyond what a stranger would expect. They then assume a variegated and beautiful dress, scarcely yielding in colours or perfume to any fields in the kingdom; and being of great extent, they afford a prospect of riches and plenty equalled by no other of the Western Isles.

James Macdonald (1811)

Ploughing, Kilkenneth, Tiree

Cattle on machair, Balemartine, Tiree

It may be the presence of stock that encourages plants such as orchids, but the real display of machair flowers is greatly enhanced by another agricultural activity; cultivation. This requires the control of grazing; township regulations, on the Uist machair for instance, ask for stock to be removed from unfenced areas by early May. With Uist machair often flooded in wet winters ploughing cannot begin much earlier, yet the sandy soils do dry off quickly.

Horse-drawn or cockshutt ploughs do not dig as deep as modern machines, reducing the risk of wind erosion and helping seeds to germinate. Management recommended by Environmentally Sensitive Area (ESA) schemes insist that crofters complete sowing and harrowing by mid-May, in order not to destroy the early clutches of oystercatchers and ringed plover that like to nest on bare ground exposed by the plough.

Tiree machair (nearly half of the island's area) is not normally cropped; perhaps because the crofting area further inland is fertile and less rocky, and so more easily ploughed. Cultivation has all but ceased in Barra, Harris and Lewis but it is a requirement of any crofter entering the Uists ESA that 15% or more of the machair share is cropped. Traditionally the area was cultivated on a 2 or 3 year rotation so that no more than half the arable machair will come under the plough at any one time.

With generous amounts of seaweed (the ESA recommends 40 tonnes per hectare), lime-rich machair soils are relatively productive yet they can be rather low in some essential nutrients and trace elements such as copper, cobalt and manganese. In the past livestock were able to make up some of this deficiency while grazing on the hills in summer, but now the animals tend to be kept in fenced areas around the croft so mineral supplements may be required.

Nutrients wash out easily from sandy soils,  so artificial fertilisers tend to be ineffective; this limits the crops that can be grown. Only the older strains of small oats and rye will thrive, the latter coping particularly well with the dry conditions as it has strong stalks that resist the wind. Small oats grow quite well in competition with wild flowers which - if the crop is intended as anything other than cattle fodder - would otherwise be condemned as weeds. It is, therefore, not practical to consider expensive herbicide treatment. Early in the season, cereal crops are dominated by corn marigold or charlock, with bugloss, field pansy and cornsalad.

In the first year of fallow, wild pansy, poppies, creeping buttercup and storksbill can flower, clover and red fescue coming through in the second year.

Kilpheder, South Uist

15

# Summer

. . . About the first of June when the cattle are put upon it, it is all over as white as a cloth, with daisies, and white clover. In that season, there may be seen pasturing upon it at once, about 1000 black cattle, 2000 sheep and 300 horses intermixed with immense flocks of lapwings and green plovers.

Reverend Dr John Walker (1764)

16

The Atlantic shores of the Highlands and Islands are a patchwork of beaches, sand dunes, grassland, croftland, wetlands and lochs. Such a range of opportunities for wildlife is so much more enhanced by the way the people manage the land. Rotating the cultivation of the machair year by year provides regular opportunities for annual plants to seed and re-establish. This helps create the spectacular displays of flowers for which the machair is well known. Tiree alone can boast over 500 species of wild plants.

Cultivated machair also has greater numbers and variety of invertebrates. Earthworms, snails, grasshoppers, flies, spiders and harvestmen are all numerous on machair but there are relatively few butterflies and moths; meadow brown, common blues and small tortoiseshell butterflies are most common with dark arches and common rustic being the most widespread moths. The belted beauty is an interesting machair moth - the females being flightless - and one theory is that they might have reached offshore islands on rafts of dead wood. Various bumble bees, including one or two Hebridean specialities, are common over machair grassland.

**Belted beauty moth**

# Birds

Corncrake

The Hebrides have become the last British stronghold of the corncrake with most occurring in Lewis, the Uists and Barra, and Tiree. Long ago people believed corncrakes spent the winter under the ice but we now know that, in May, they arrive from Africa. Rarely seen but characteristically noisy, they seek early cover in iris beds until the hayfields grow tall enough. Although special measures are included for them in the ESAs of the Uists, Shetland and the Argyll Islands, corncrakes tend to be birds of the croftland and hay meadows more than machair grassland and crops.

Corn buntings still thrive on cultivated machair in the Uists and Tiree, but are on the verge of extinction on mainland farms. Twite is another characteristic bird of the machair, replacing the linnet found elsewhere, while the rare little tern often forsakes the foreshore to nest on the cultivated land.

Undoubtedly, machair is most famous for its waders. Over 25,000 pairs bred each year on machair during the 1980s, some 6,000 in Tiree alone, with over 17,000 in the Uists and Barra. The other machair areas, in Orkney, Shetland and on the Irish or Scottish mainland, are less rich.

The most numerous wader is the peewit or lapwing, a bird now increasingly rare on intensive farmland on the mainland. In the Uists, lapwing breed in the highest densities among the dune slacks and on drier grasslands (up to 85 pairs per km$^2$). There are fewer in damp machair and fewest on dry cultivated machair and croftland; in Tiree lapwing densities are lower still.

Dunlin are more specific in their breeding requirements preferring the tufted vegetation of wet machair to conceal their nests. A record density of some 300 pairs per km$^2$ was recorded from one area of South Uist in the 1980s, when some 40% of the British population were to be found on the machairs of the Uists and Tiree alone.

Redshank and snipe prefer the taller vegetation of marshes and wetlands but since the latter tend to be pretty secretive their numbers are likely to have been underestimated. With longer beaks, redshank and snipe (together with dunlin) can probe deeper into wet ground to find food.

It is the oystercatcher and ringed plover that are most dependent upon crofting practices. Both will nest on dry cultivated machair and up to 400 pairs per km$^2$ of ringed plover have been recorded on ploughed land or recent fallow in the Uists; all together amounting to nearly one-third of the total breeding population in Britain. Ringed plover will also nest on shingle beaches or bare ground, where their camouflaged eggs are best concealed; they also like the broken runways on The Reef in Tiree.

Lapwing

Twite

Dunlin

Redshank

Ringed plover

# Autumn

'The crops in North Uist and Benbecula, but especially South Uist, are exposed to a very singular misfortune; being sometimes entirely destroyed by the vast flocks of wild geese, which haunt these islands. This bird is never seen in the south of Scotland except in winter but in these islands it hatches and resides all the year round. . .'

Reverend Dr John Walker (1764)

Storm-cast, rotting seaweed shelters so many invertebrates that in autumn and winter the shores and beaches near the machair become important feeding grounds for waders. The oystercatchers and redshank breeding in the Uists move further south for the winter but are replaced by birds that have bred in Iceland. The local ringed plover remain in the Hebrides all winter - the only non-migratory population of this species in the world - while the smaller Arctic birds leap-frog across them to winter in Africa. Northern dunlin, on the other hand, are 20% larger than local dunlin, so birds from Greenland take over for the winter forcing the Hebridean ones to move further south. Turnstones from Greenland and Arctic

20

Canada also overwinter in the Hebrides. Whimbrel, sanderling and purple sandpiper come from Iceland; bar-tailed godwit and grey plover from Siberia. Golden plover are abundant too, some of which breed locally. We do not know if local snipe stay for the winter but with so many taken by estate shooting parties their numbers must be topped up with migrants from further north.

Now that scythes have been replaced by modern machinery, crofters are encouraged - by ESA payments - to delay cutting their hay until August, and to cut from the centre of the field outwards, so that corncrakes can escape from the mower blades into neighbouring crops. The corn is cut in September or early October, having allowed the wild flowers to set seed. Where the fields are too small for binders or balers, the corn may still be tied in sheaves, then stooked before being taken back to the stack yard to be used as winter fodder; some will be threshed as seed for next season.

Later in October, barnacle and white-fronted geese arrive from Greenland, with whooper swans from Iceland. These wildfowl, along with the resident greylag geese, like to feed on the stubble. Recently, the barnacle geese tend to have forsaken some undisturbed offshore islands to frequent improved pasture. Their name derives from an ancient belief that they spent the summer as goose barnacles; stalked, marine crustaceans that look not dissimilar, although very much smaller, of course. Indeed, the Gaelic name for the geese and the barnacles is the same; `giodhran'.

Barnacle geese

# Greylag geese

Greylag geese now breed in several parts of northern Scotland and the Inner Hebrides. There has always been a resident population of birds in the Uists which are reckoned to be the original pure, native stock.

Recent counts indicate about 100 greylags on Colonsay, some 700 on Coll with a similar number on Lewis and Harris, 2,000 on Tiree and about 4,000 on the Uists. Although wildfowlers are permitted to shoot them in winter, the goose numbers are increasing slightly each year. These flocks do not compare with the huge numbers wintering on the mainland and on Islay but, in a crofting context, the damage they might do can still be significant. In some parts of the Uists, for instance, geese can deprive sheep of the first flush of grass on some reseeded pastures in spring, or might flatten or graze ripening corn just prior to harvest in the autumn.

Since cultivation is so important to the conservation interests of machair, geese cannot be allowed to threaten its continuation. In the Uists, a Goose Management Committee has been formed, bringing together crofters, estates, the local council and agencies like the Scottish Office Agriculture, Environment and Fisheries Department (SOAEFD) and Scottish Natural Heritage. Not only does this committee organise regular counts but it assesses complaints and organises goose scaring. Their role is to minimise pressure on crofting especially during harvest time while still retaining a viable breeding population of pure-bred Scottish greylags. A similar committee has now been formed in Tiree.

Greylag goose

# Keeping the balance

In summer the cows and milk sheep are sent to the glens, which are covered with heath and hard grasses, sedges and rushes, because the part consisting of soft grass is not in general sufficient for their maintenance during the whole year . . . Black cattle are small but well-shaped. They are covered with a thick and long pile to enable them to resist the winter's cold - a good pile is considered one of the best qualifications of a cow

William Macgillivray's diaries (1818)

Golf Course, Scarista machair, Harris

Sheep grazing on Kilpheder machair, South Uist

Low-intensity land use as practised on the machair is as important for plants and animals as it is to the local people. This distinctive mix of culture, landscape and wildlife generates tourism; so good crofting and nature conservation are a highly viable combination and both are essential to the economy of the islands.

Cattle have long been an important part of the machair system. They do not graze as closely as sheep, taking not only the less appetizing species but also the less attractive portions; more stem, seed heads, dead vegetable material, rushes, cotton grass and other less tasty plants. Cattle, therefore, improve the quality of the grassland for other grazers as well as for wildlife.

In addition, cattle play a part in shaping the machair landscape. Tussocks, for example, are good habitats for invertebrates and thus provide both food and nest sites for birds. Waders have been known to use hoof prints as nest-cups, while some ringed plovers try to conceal their nest beside a dry cow pat.

24

The break-up of coarse plants (such as iris root systems) further opens up and improves the pasture, with any bare patches created being good for invertebrates and as seed beds for annual plants. Dung contains the seeds and grain necessary to regenerate the ground while also adding nutrients and humus.

Too much bare ground eroded (or poached) by stock can, however, encourage invasive weeds, such as ragwort. Sheep will eat this when it is young whereas cattle find it poisonous. While more environmentally-friendly than large numbers of sheep, cattle are quite labour-intensive. It may be the cheapest option to grow winter fodder on the machair, but cattle still need to be fed daily in the winter and even housed in bad weather. If not enough fodder is grown locally feed would have to be bought in, or the cattle even sent off to overwinter on the mainland. This loss of cropped land and of winter dung from the ground is detrimental to any good machair system. Artificial fertilisers reduce the variety of plants and tend to favour the more aggressive, but not necessarily the best, species in the grassland.

Too many sheep can break open the thin dry soils, or rub against sand banks, thus promoting erosion. An unfortunate trend in recent years has been to fence off individual apportionments of machair to confine stock all the year round. This leads to heavy grazing in summer preventing plants from flowering or setting seed and leading to less variety of species. It also removes cover for nesting and feeding birds and increases the risk of nests being trampled.

Agricultural support should be geared to helping crofters continue their already environmentally-friendly practices. Environmentally Sensitive Area schemes provide one such opportunity, where special payments promote cropping the machair, applying seaweed or dung, employing measures that favour grassland birds

and managing wetlands sympathetically. There is also support for townships to construct sand-blow fencing and to plant marram against erosion.

Oldshore Beg, Sutherland

# Alien introductions

The mammals that have naturally colonised the Northern Isles, the Inner and Outer Hebrides are limited; pygmy shrews, field voles, Orkney vole, mice and rats, otters, red deer and seals. It is probably the absence of land predators, including foxes and stoats, that has resulted in such high numbers of ground-nesting birds, such as waders and corncrakes. Feral cats can be a nuisance, as can a more recent introduction, ferrets. They were originally brought to the island to control the rabbits, themselves imported by humans, as a potential source of food. Tiree and Berneray (off North Uist) still have no rabbits although the latter will be at risk of invasion over the new causeway.

**Hedgehog**

Rabbit damage on machair

There is no justification for introducing any wild animal to an island. Ferrets have never succeeded in controlling rabbits. Rats, cats and mink have wiped out many bird colonies. Mink reached the Uists from Lewis and Harris in the mid 1990s and are spreading. Hedgehogs - introduced to the Uists in the 1970s - are not munching as many garden slugs as they were expected to, but also find wader eggs appealing. Recent studies by SNH and the RSPB have demonstrated serious declines in wader numbers in South Uist and Benbecula due to hedgehog predation, while North Uist too is now being invaded by this prickly predator; they are also present in Coll and Tiree. Natura designations in Uist have drawn substantial European funding to protect the internationally important concentrations of breeding waders from mink. A trapping programme is now under way and it is hoped that the hedgehog problem can be similarly addressed.

# The future

Many examples of machair have been designated Sites of Special Scientific Interest, Special Protection Areas or Special Areas of Conservation (under the European Directives) or as nature reserves. This helps promote appropriate management for the benefit of wildlife. But there are more major problems. With global warming adding to a gradual rise in sea level and an increase in Atlantic storms, the threat of erosion is greater than ever. Rabbits, and stock, can add to dune erosion, while dumping of rubbish, uncontrolled vehicle/caravan access to machair and dune buggies or motorbikes tearing up sand slopes can create local problems. Yet still, there are few beaches more lovely and unspoilt than those of the Northern and Western Isles; all very important for the local tourist trade (though perhaps midges, cool winds and cold seas help make sure they never become over popular!)

Sand dunes, Luskentyre, Harris

Rubbish dumping on machair

Marram should never be abused. It should be cut only for thatching, or for transplanting in dune stabilisation works, within strict guidelines, in moderation and well back from any actively-eroding edge. Every opportunity should be taken to prevent blow-outs, and any replanting should be undertaken as sensitively as possible. Marram is always a better solution than unsightly, less effective and expensive, man-made defences.

27

Left over from the Ice Age, shingle beaches form a vital defence from eroding waves. The preservation of this natural barrier is very important and it should only be interfered with in exceptional circumstances; and certainly not for commercial uses. Kelp beds are another important protection so any offshore exploitation by the seaweed industry should be discouraged, The winter cast of tangle not only provides vital protection against storms and erosion but is also essential to the maintenance of the machair and traditional land use.

Machair is a unique and dynamic habitat. It is one of the best examples of a distinctive culture with a finely-tuned land use

successfully supporting an extremely rich wildlife resource. Generations of local folk have understood enough of the system to use it to their advantage, to cherish it for their very survival and to pass on this knowledge to their children. But pressures of modern living threaten to undermine that ancient balance. We still need to have a better understanding of machair and its wildlife in order that the needs of the people living there can be provided for, since machair without people would be a very much poorer place. In accepting that sand blow will always be a necessary feature of life on the Atlantic fringe, we need to be aware of the most effective ways to contain it so that the experience of Skara Brae's deserted village may remain a feature of prehistory.

Highland Cattle grazing on the Machair

## Also in Scotland's Living Landscapes series

If you have enjoyed Mountains why not find out more about Scotland's distinctive habitats in our Scotland's Living Landscapes series. Each 'landscape' is a dynamic environment supporting a wealth of plants and animals, whose lives are woven inextricably together. The colourfully illustrated booklets explore these complex relationships simply and concisely, and explain why they are important and what needs to be done to protect them for the future.

### Sea Lochs

Featuring dramatic underwater photography, this booklet tells why Scotland's sea lochs are so special to people living around their shores and to the magnificent wildlife that depends on their sheltered waters.
Sue Scott
ISBN 1 85397 246 0 pbk 24pp £3.00

### Firths

Firths lie at the heart of Scottish life: they support our economy, house most of our population, and provide a precious home for wildlife. Discover the magic of our unsung firths and the efforts being made to secure their future.
Steve Atkins
ISBN 1 85397 271 1 pbk 36pp £3.50

### Coasts

Scotland has nearly 12,000km of coastline, much of it remote, unspoilt and strikingly beautiful. Learn all about this changing environment, the unique habitats, landforms and wildlife and the many pressures they face.
George Lees & Kathy Duncan
ISBN 1 85397 003 4 pbk 28pp £3.00

### Boglands

Bogland is one of Britain's most undervalued habitats. This booklet challenges the conventional view of boglands and rewards its reader with vivid images of the colourful and intriguing wildlife of bogs.
Richard Lindsay
ISBN 1 85397 120 2 pbk 20pp £3.95

### Soils

As all gardeners know, what grows on the surface depends on what's beneath their feet. Indeed soils are home to a all sorts of animals as well as plants. This booklet relates the story of our soils to the landscapes we see everyday.
Andrew Taylor & Stephen Nortcliff
ISBN 1 85397 223 1 pbk 24pp £2.50

### Kelp Forests

An essential introduction to this hidden kingdom. Discover the variety of plants and animals which live in the 'forests', find out why kelp forests are so important in Scottish waters and how healthy kelp forests help to prevent coastal erosion.
Ian Fuller
ISBN 1 85397 014X pbk 44pp £3.95

### Grasslands

Grasslands form an important part of our natural heritage and this booklet looks at how they provide a vital habitat for birds, butterflies, animals and plants.
Stephen Ward & Jane MacKintosh
ISBN 1 85397 070 0 pbk 48pp £3.95

### Mountains

Two thirds of Scotland is covered by mountains and wild uplands, which straddle geological and climatic boundaries to give us several distinct mountain areas. These special landscapes and their wildlife are vulnerable to intensive use and demand the highest standards of stewardship.
Mark Wrightham
ISBN 1 85397 326 2 pbk 40pp £4.95

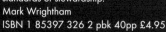

# SNH Publications Order Form:
## Living Landscapes Series

| Title | Price | Quantity |
|---|---|---|
| Sea Lochs | £3.00 | |
| Firths | £3.50 | |
| Machair | £3.00 | |
| Coasts | £3.00 | |
| Boglands | £3.95 | |
| Soils | £2.50 | |
| Kelp Forests | £3.95 | |
| Grasslands | £4.95 | |
| Mountains | £4.95 | |

Postage and packaging: free of charge within the UK.

A standard charge of £2.95 will be applied to all orders from the EU.

Elsewhere a standard charge of £5.50 will apply.

Please complete in **BLOCK CAPITALS**

Name _____

Address _____

_____

_____

Post Code

Type of Credit Card   VISA ☐   MasterCard ☐

Name of card holder _____

Card Number

☐☐☐☐  ☐☐☐☐  ☐☐☐☐  ☐☐☐☐

Expiry Date  ☐☐ ☐☐

Send order and cheque made payable to Scottish Natural Heritage to:

Scottish Natural Heritage, Design and Publications, Battleby, Redgorton, Perth PH1 3EW

E-mail: pubs@snh.gov.uk   www.snh.org.uk

We may want to send you details of other SNH publications. Please tick the box below if you do not want this. We will not pass your details to anyone else.

I do not wish to receive information on SNH publications ☐

Please add my name to the mailing list for the   SNH Magazine ☐

Publications Catalogue ☐